STARS OF NASCAR

Kasey KAHNE

BY MATT DOEDEN

Reading Consultant:
Barbara J. Fox
Reading Specialist
North Carolina State University

Content Consultant:
Betty L. Carlan
Research Librarian
International Motorsports Hall of Fame
Talladega, Alabama

Capstone
press®

Mankato, Minnesota

Blazers is published by Capstone Press,
151 Good Counsel Drive, P.O. Box 669, Mankato, Minnesota 56002.
www.capstonepress.com

Library of Congress Cataloging-in-Publication Data
Doeden, Matt.
    Kasey Kahne / by Matt Doeden.
    p. cm. — (Blazers. Stars of NASCAR)
    Summary: "Explores the life and racing career of NASCAR Sprint Cup star
Kasey Kahne" — Provided by publisher.
    Includes bibliographical references and index.
    ISBN-13: 978-1-4296-1980-6 (hardcover)
    ISBN-10: 1-4296-1980-5 (hardcover)
    1. Kahne, Kasey, 1980 — Juvenile literature. 2. Stock car drivers — United States
— Biography — Juvenile literature. I. Title.
GV1032.K34D64 2009
796.72092 — dc22
[B]   2007052194

Essential content terms are **bold** and are defined on the spread where they first appear.

Editorial Credits
Abby Czeskleba, editor; Bobbi J. Wyss, designer; Jo Miller, photo researcher

Photo Credits
AP Images/Bob Jordan, 18–19; Chris Gardner, 29; J. Pat Carter, 24–25; Matt
    Slocum, 23; Terry Renna, 8–9
Corbis/GT Images/George Tiedemann, cover (Kahne)
Getty Images for NASCAR/Rusty Jarrett, 26–27
Getty Images Inc./Craig Jones, 4–5; Rusty Jarrett, 20–21; Streeter Lecka, 6–7;
    Wire Image/Al Messerschmidt, 17
M&M Photos/Matt Sublett, 10–11, 12–13, 14–15
The Sharpe Image/Sam Sharpe, 16
Shutterstock/Anastasios Kandris (speed and racing icons, throughout); Bocos Benedict
    (abstract digital background, throughout); Rzymu (flag background, throughout)
Zuma Press/Cal Sport Media/John Pyle, cover (car)

1 2 3 4 5 6 13 12 11 10 09 08

TABLE OF CONTENTS

THE LONGEST RACE

Only 32 laps remained in the 2006 Coca-Cola 600. Kasey Kahne was in third place at Lowe's Motor Speedway. He kept perfect control over his red number 9 car.

Kasey drove to the outside part of the track. He sailed past Jimmie Johnson. Kasey moved to the inside part of the track. He inched past Carl Edwards. Kasey was in the lead!

TRACK FACT!

Kasey took the lead with just 29 laps left in the race.

Johnson and Edwards tried to catch him, but Kasey was too fast. He shouted as he took the *checkered flag*. He'd won one of NASCAR's biggest races!

TRACK FACT!

At 600 miles (966 km), the Coca Cola 600 is NASCAR's longest race. Drivers make 400 laps around the 1.5-mile (2.4-km) track.

checkered flag — a flag used to signal when the first car has crossed the finish line

Kasey driving a sprint car

A LOVE OF RACING

Kasey Kahne was born April 10, 1980, in Enumclaw, Washington. He started racing at a young age. In 1994, he began racing **sprint cars** at local speedways.

TRACK FACT!

By age 16, Kasey had won two sprint car championships.

sprint car — a small car built for racing on short dirt tracks

Kasey's skill at handling sprint cars got him a lot of attention. In 2000, he started driving **Silver Crown cars**. That year, Kasey won the Silver Crown Series Rookie of the Year award.

Silver Crown car — a front-engine car that is driven in 100-lap or 100-mile (161-km) races without making pit stops

Kasey also drove **midget cars**.
In 2000, he won the United States
Auto Club (USAC) Midget Series
championship. He also earned the
Driver of the Year award.

Kasey racing a midget car

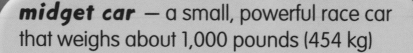

midget car — a small, powerful race car
that weighs about 1,000 pounds (454 kg)

TRACK FACT!

In 2001, Kasey won four races in the USAC Midget Series.

In 2002, Kasey started racing in the **Busch Series**. He drove in 20 races that season. He earned his first win at the last race of the 2003 season.

Busch Series — NASCAR's second-highest level of competition where drivers gain experience before moving on to the Cup Series

NASCAR STAR

In 2004, Kasey began racing in the *Cup Series*. He replaced Bill Elliott as the driver of the number 9 car. Kasey didn't win a race that year, but he finished in second place five times.

Cup Series — NASCAR's highest level of competition

TRACK FACT!

Kasey won the Cup Series
Rookie of the Year award in 2004.

Things got even better for Kasey in 2005. He earned two back-to-back **poles**. He also celebrated his first Cup win at Richmond International Speedway. Kasey finished in the top-10 a total of eight times that season.

pole — the inside spot in the front row of cars at the beginning of a race

Kasey made the 2006 **Chase for the Cup** in the final regular-season race. He knocked defending Cup champion Tony Stewart out of the Chase. Kasey finished eighth in the standings.

TRACK FACT!

Kasey had six Cup wins in 2006. He won more races than any other driver that year.

Chase for the Cup — the last 10 races of the Cup Series in which the top drivers battle for the championship

KASEY TODAY

Kasey's 2007 season was awful. Something seemed to go wrong every week. One week, he crashed. The next, his engine broke. He struggled to a disappointing 19th-place finish in the Cup Series standings.

Even though he had a bad season in 2007, Kasey is still one of NASCAR's rising stars. His winning smile and strong driving skills make him a hit with fans and other drivers.

TRACK FACT!

In 2007, fans voted Kasey as one of the top-10 most popular drivers in the Cup Series.

27

CUP CAREER STATISTICS

Kasey Kahne's Cup Statistics

Year	Races	Wins	Poles	Top-5	Top-10	Winnings
2004	36	0	4	13	14	$4,759,022
2005	36	1	2	5	8	$4,874,838
2006	36	6	6	12	19	$6,204,222
2007	36	0	2	1	8	$5,148,469
Career	**144**	**7**	**14**	**31**	**49**	**$20,986,551**

GLOSSARY

Busch Series (BUSH SEER-eez) — NASCAR's second-highest level of competition where drivers gain experience before moving on to the Cup Series; in 2008, the series became the Nationwide Series.

Chase for the Cup — the last 10 races of the Cup season in which the top 12 drivers battle for the championship

checkered flag (CHEK-urd FLAG) — a flag used to signal when the first car has crossed the finish line

Cup Series — NASCAR's highest level of competition; the series has been known as the Winston Cup and the Nextel Cup; it is now called the Sprint Cup.

midget car (MIJ-it KAR) — a small, powerful race car with a four-cylinder engine

pole — the inside spot in the front row of cars at the beginning of a race; drivers earn the pole by having the best qualifying time.

rookie (RUK-ee) — a first-year driver

Silver Crown car (SIL-vur KROUN KAR) — a front-engine car that is driven in 100-lap or 100-mile (161-km) races without pit stops

sprint car (SPRINT KAR) — a small car built for racing on short dirt tracks

READ MORE

Dayton, Connor. *Kasey Kahne.* NASCAR Champions. New York: PowerKids Press, 2008.

Doeden, Matt. *Behind the Wheel.* NASCAR Racing. Mankato, Minn.: Capstone Press, 2008.

Eagen, Rachel. *NASCAR.* Automania! New York: Crabtree, 2007.

INTERNET SITES

FactHound offers a safe, fun way to find Internet sites related to this book. All of the sites on FactHound have been researched by our staff.

Here's how:
1. Visit *www.facthound.com*
2. Choose your grade level.
3. Type in this book ID **1429619805** for age-appropriate sites. You may also browse subjects by clicking on letters, or by clicking on pictures and words.
4. Click on the **Fetch It** button.

FactHound will fetch the best sites for you!

INDEX